Modern Artists

Kricke

John Anthony Thwaites

Kricke

Harry N. Abrams, Inc., Publishers, New York

For Gitta and Barnabas

Library of Congress Catalog No. 64-18893

A hand moves across the paper. The movement is slow and certain, with a continuous circling rhythm. It leaves trails behind, as the charcoal makes transparent, dark-edged signs, like clouds. At first the hand seems driven by unconscious forces. Then it stops. The motion changes, becomes short, decided, staccato. Hard black accents come. Then a line, irregular, from top to bottom. Then another. In the dialogue between the artist and his drawing, the subconscious demands the comment of the conscious eye. Now the composition pulls itself together. It acquires a focus and a personality, as the line, by its rhythm, defines the relationships. After that the circling begins once more. As modulations broaden out, the surface now starts to dissolve. Structure is transformed to space and movement, each of them dependent on the other. The drawing, though, is not constructive and not mathematical, more like the nervous system of the human body, organic and electrical at once. The tensions correspond with those of nature, but they have travelled through a human mind – 'La nature vue à travers un tempérament'.

The experience of the sculptor Norbert Kricke at the drawing-board. In all the visual arts, drawing is primary. It is the point at which the alternating current of the conscious and subconscious has its start. The creative process begins here. Today, however, the relationship between the drawing and the finished work has changed. With Matisse or Picasso, the path leads not so much from sketch to painting as the other way. A generation on, with Pollock and de Kooning, the sketch is both the start and finish. In sculpture, *mutatis mutandis*, the same thing is true. The 'sculptor's drawing' no longer exists. And no solid object can emerge from such a drawing (Nos. 12 and 42). The problem has changed now. The question is: how can a conception like this take on a three- or rather, four-dimensional form?

The 'decline of the old cultural canon'[1] shows perhaps most clearly in our sense of time. We have less feeling for eternal values than for eternal flux of change. The absolute has been replaced by the comparative, the static by the dynamic. Not only the arts and philosophy, our economic systems, our technology, our social life all show the change. Is it surprising then that sculpture has been revolutionised? Brancusi, Gabo, Calder, Giacometti, much of Moore are unthinkable in any other period. The same is true of the young generation, which Kricke represents almost alone in Germany. Here the very medium has changed. In all its history sculpture was the art of mass. Today it is the art of space.

Kricke's first space-sculptures date from 1949, two years after he left the Berlin Academy. Of contemporary work developing in Britain and America he knew nothing at all. He was simply fascinated by the open structure of the armature before the clay is

1. Drawing, 1963 (pp. 7–9)

built up on it, and began again from there. No. 2 dates from this early period. Three linear forms, black, white and grey, run into one another. A series of right-angles placed at different levels in the air, their only connections are rhythm and space. The lines function not as a structure but as lines of force. They cut through space, compress it and articulate it, building up the architecture of the work.

'Architecture' not as static volume, but the thrust and counter-thrust in a steel skeleton. Yet even here there is a basic difference. 'We are living increasingly in a dead, technical kind of space arrived at by mathematical calculation. Western man's vital sense of space is steadily atrophying, and here is a danger not only intellectual but biological as well, for it means that his living space and breathing space are being destroyed from within.'[2] It is the lost, living sense of space which sculpture such as this restores. The rhythm of No. 2, though, is a static one. Space rises and falls over the base-plane like the breath of a sleeping body. Nos. 3 and 4 show something very different, which one finds in the work from 1950 on. That thing is speed. Speed in the sense of movement beyond the biologically possible: everything which we experience from the automobile to space-rocketry. The speed which is our scale for cosmic measurement. It is more than half a century since the dynamic concept made both space and time obsolete for natural science.[3] As soon as one can feel in four dimensions it is obvious that the geometry of Kricke's work is non-Euclidean. The lines form no imaginary planes, the planes no structure. The forms are forms of speed, like smoke-trails from a jet. The sculptures exist in the concept of space-time.

In this period they are also coloured. What part can colour play? From the start of the modern movement there have been experiments with polychrome. 'With the polychroming,' wrote Henri Laurens, 'I wanted to make it possible for the sculpture to control its own light.'[4] Without the paint, the light would swallow the lines of Kricke's work. But it has more than a protective function here. Each one of the component rhythms needs a different colour. In the big sculpture No. 5, for example, the lower part is almost terracotta. The movement here is slow, rising and falling, earthbound but generous. The contrasting angle which shoots up seems speeded by the fact that it is white. The simplicity of linear structure, which comes close to the schematic, is enriched again by colour as a counterpoint.

When these sculptures were made, few understood what the sculptor was getting at. But since then, the event of Sputnik, the Moon shots, the Venus Probe and the first manned satellites, has given everyone a different sense of space. And suddenly the sculptures

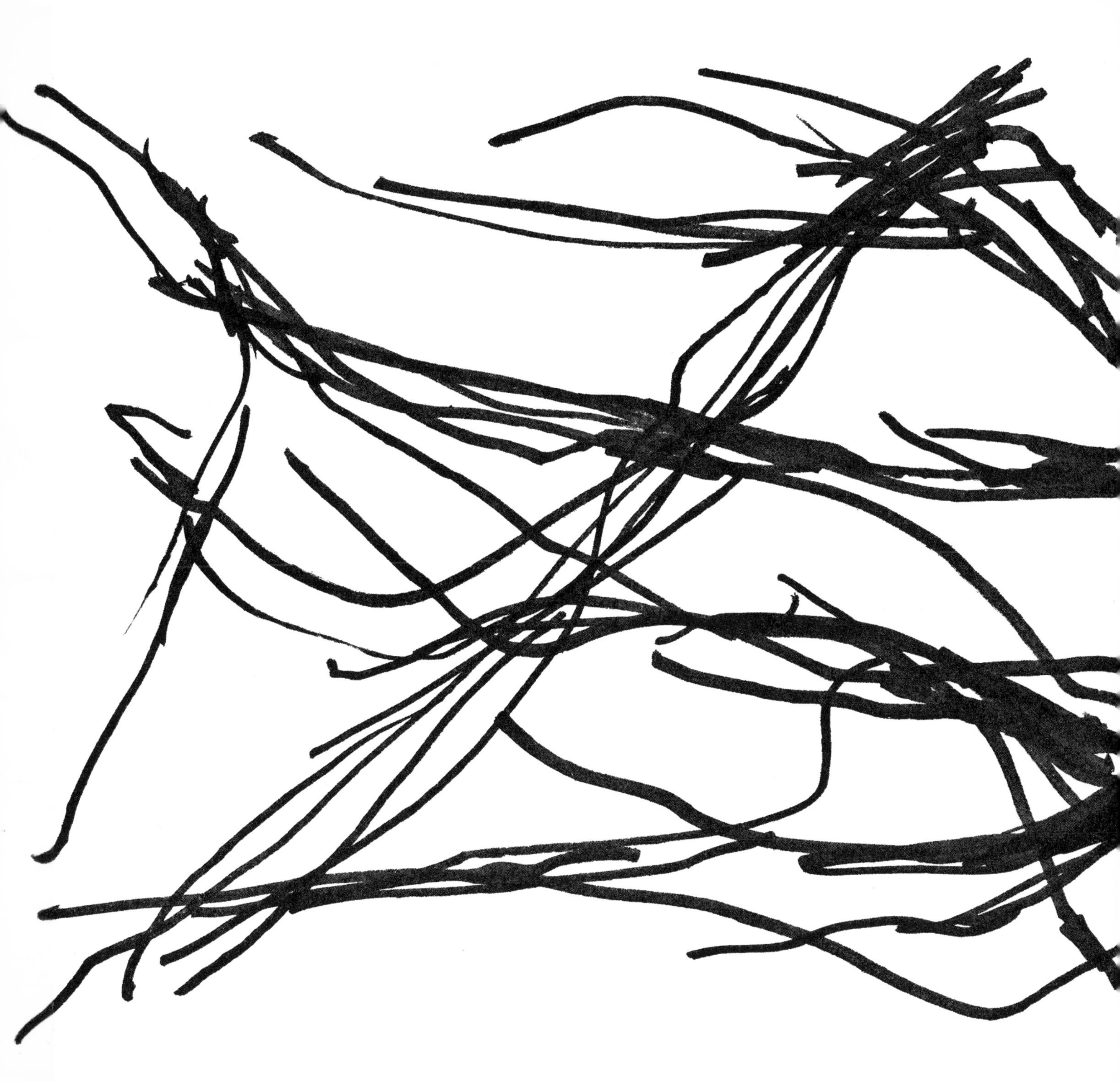

are no more a riddle. An interesting effect of these dynamics can be seen in No. 8. This is based on the contrast of vertical with horizontal. The basic principle of Classic art. Here white as a colour emphasizes the repose. Yet this stillness is the product of a set of movements and counter-movements. No. 7 in contrast, of two years earlier, is as static as the early work.

The next development showed its first signs in 1952 in No. 9, a small piece coloured green and at the time an isolated work. Here a new principle comes in. The straight line gives way to the curve. At first this seems to show an inclination to biology, away from physics, which the colour (for Kricke unique) would stress. But the rhythm is spatial, not linear, produced by movement, not abstracted from the natural world. With Nos. 11, 14, 15, 16, 17, some three years later, the new phase reaches its full development. The lines are bundled now and not alone, so light-protection is not needed any more. On the contrary, light changing and reflecting from the polished surfaces gives a new life and substitutes the stimulus of colour.

Of all the sculptor's works these are perhaps the easiest to 'read'. That they were greeted with cries of 'spaghetti' by some German art-historians throws an interesting light upon the gentlemen concerned. For most young people, on the other hand, these things are natural. The concentrated energy and centrifugal form are part of their known world. Still, is the inspiration from technology maybe too obvious? Is this a theme for art? That question Siegfried Giedion answered once and for all a quarter of a century ago. 'The feelings,' he wrote, 'which the contemporary world elicits have remained formless, have never met with those objects which are at once their symbols and their satisfaction. Such symbols however are vital . . . We need to discover harmonies between our own inner states and our surroundings . . . The opening-up of such new realms of feeling has always been the artist's chief mission.'[5] This does not mean that the organic elements of No. 9 get lost. One finds them again in No. 10. The rhythm slows down here. Although confined to white, paint is retained; it gives more sense of flesh and less of light. One thinks of the slow-motion documentaries about the growth of plants, or, in another time-scale, big boughs moving in the wind. In art one thinks of the mobiles of Alexander Calder. In all these, though, the movement is physical and 'accidental'. It 'represents' only itself. Kricke translates the motion back into the rhythms of a physically static piece. This gives it a symbolic character: all movement, not just the tempo of the present moment.

It would be possible to criticize the 'Balls-of-energy' (Nos. 15–17) as superficial, insufficiently transformed. Their 'legibility' could point that way. In No. 20 the movement, the scattering, has a different effect. One feels enclosed in it, a part of moving space.

3

3. Space Sculpture Yellow-White-Black, 1956 (p. 12)
4. Space Sculpture, 1952 (p. 13)
5. 'Small Liègeois' White-Terracotta, 1952

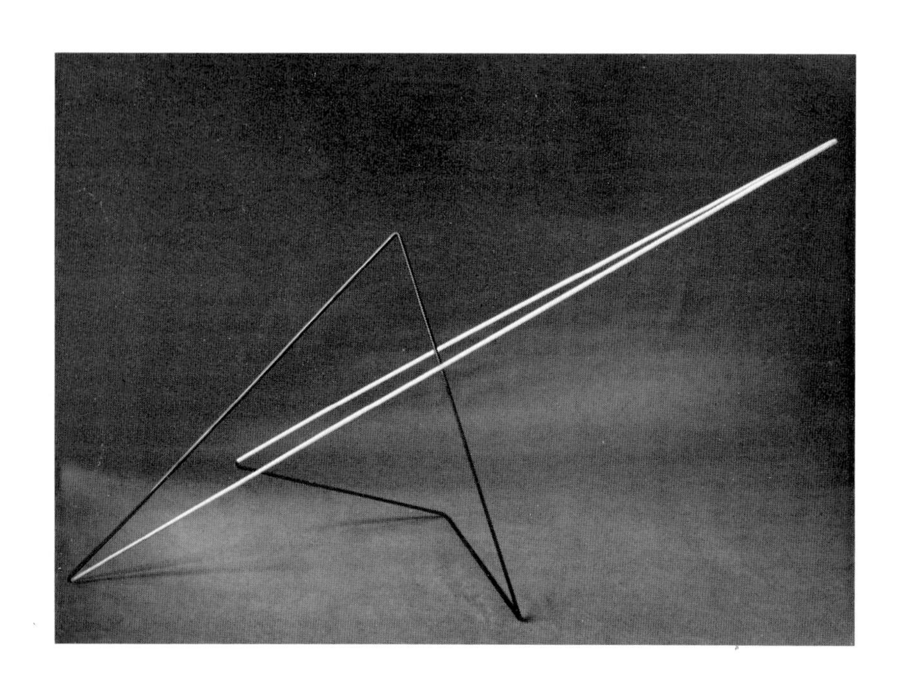

6. Space Sculpture Red, 1954

7. Small White Architectural, 1950
8. Space Sculpture White 'Temple', 1952 〉

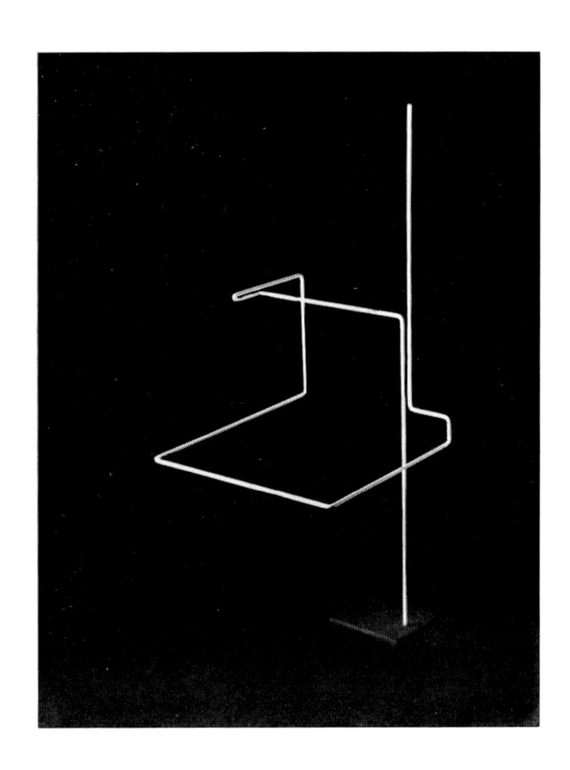

17

9. Green Curve, 1952
10. Space Sculpture White, 1955 〉

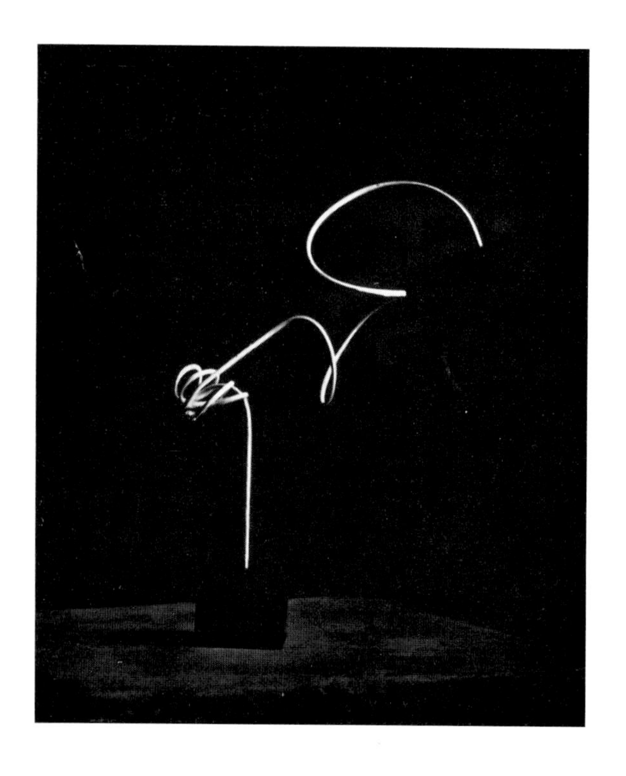

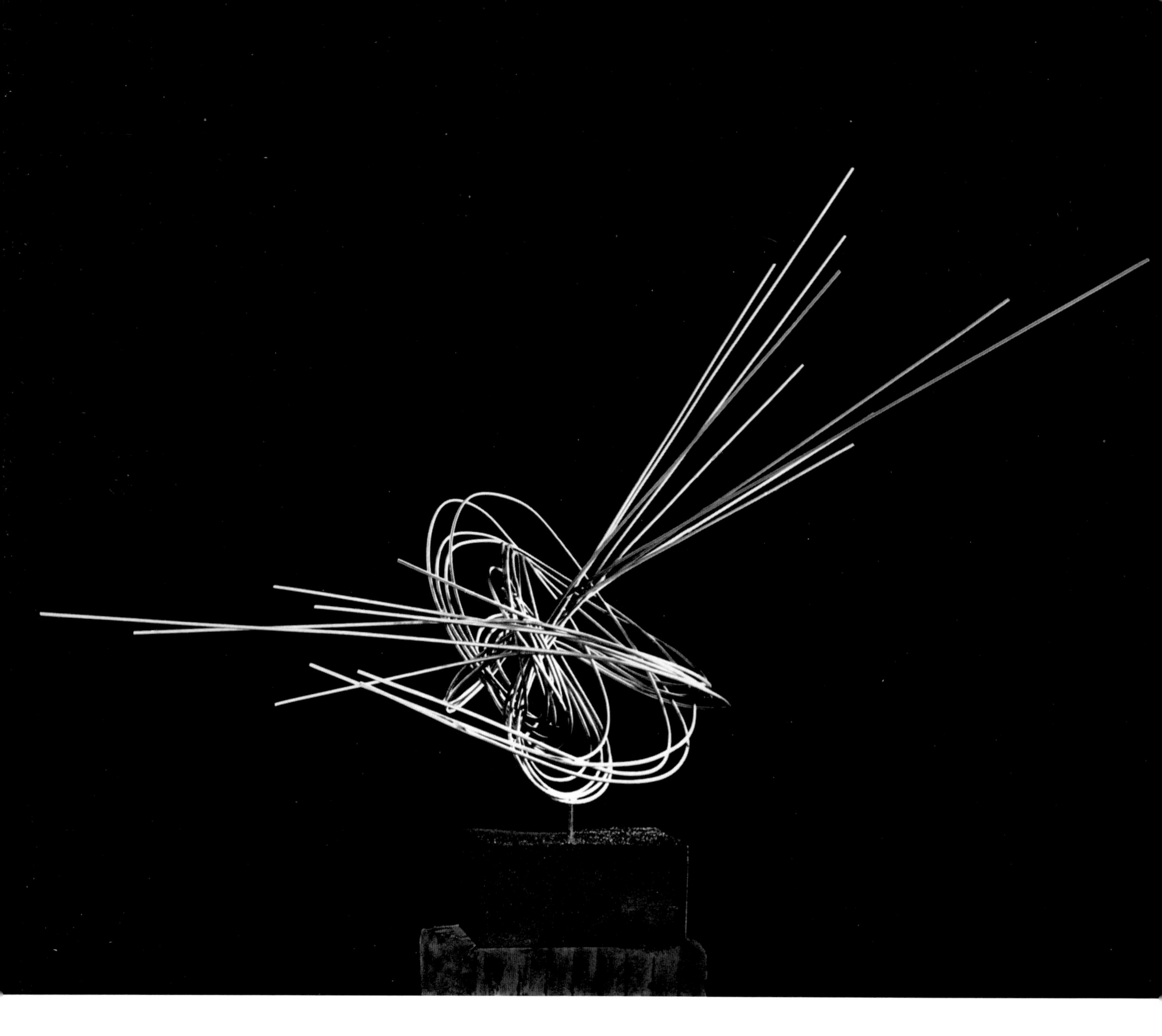

〈 11. Space Sculpture, 1955
12. Drawing, 1956

‹ 13. Drawing, 1955
14. Space Sculpture, 1955

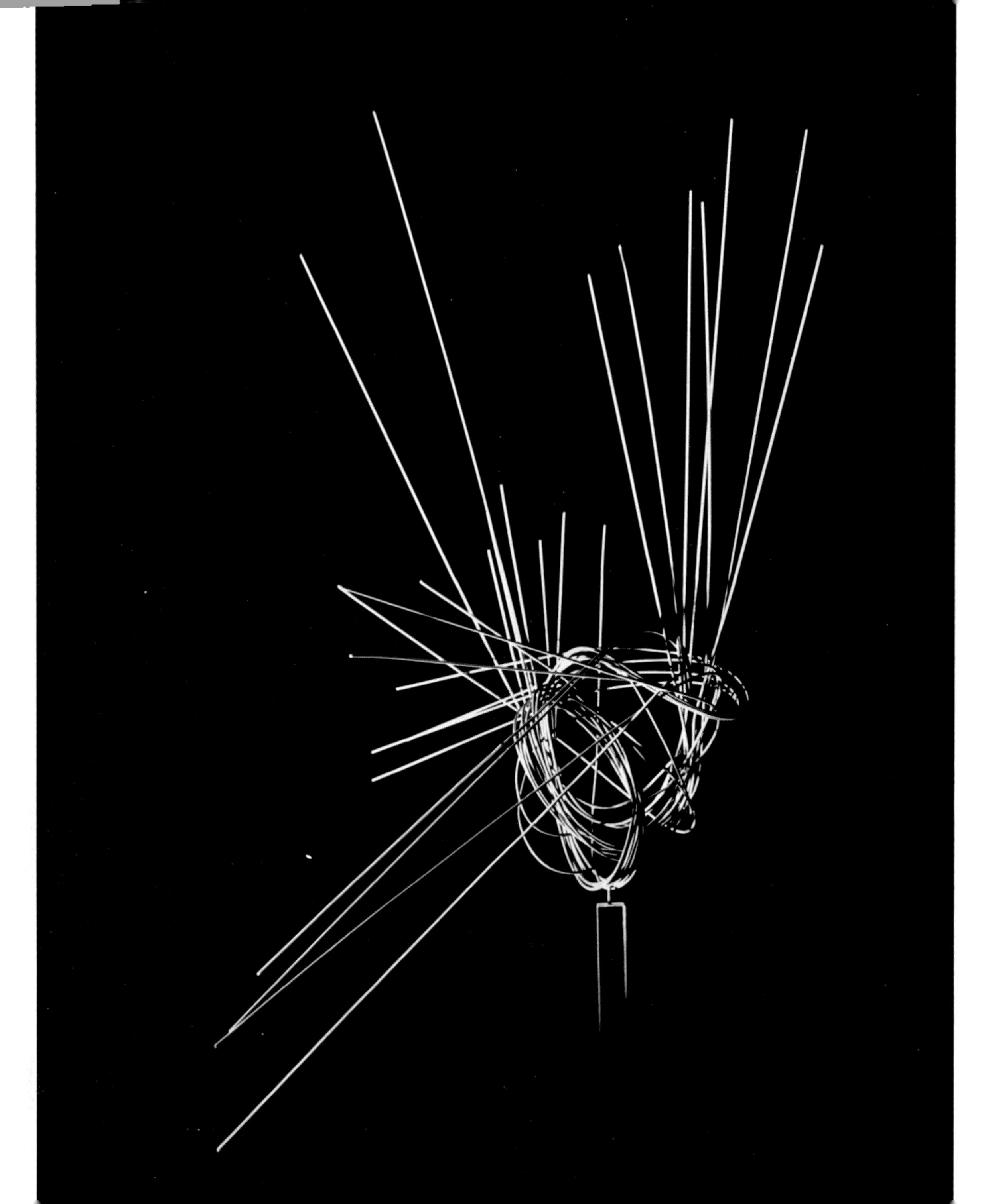

15. Space Sculpture
Grey-White, 1955–1956

16. Space Sculpture
'Hornet', 1955–1956

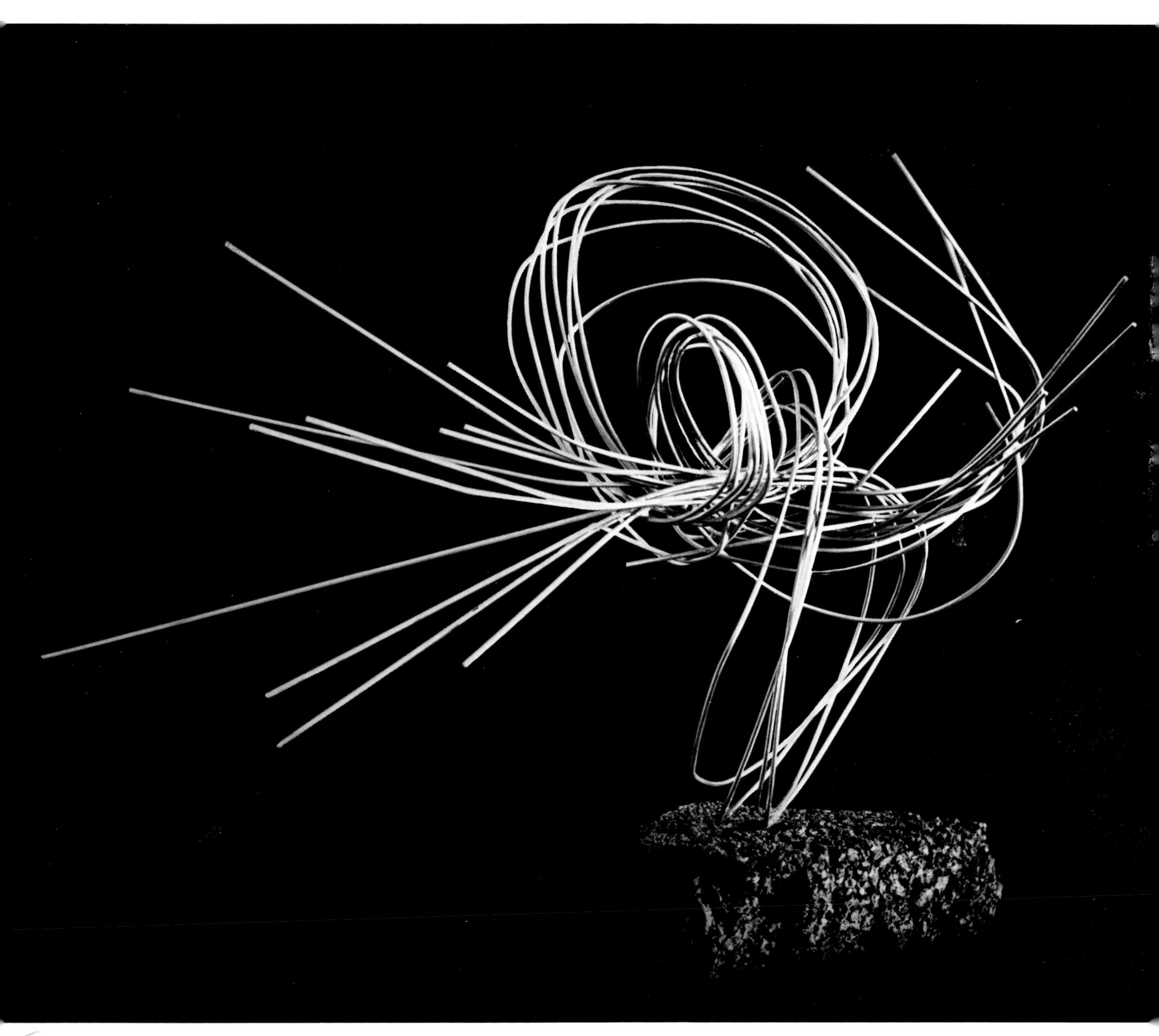

17. Space Sculpture, 1955

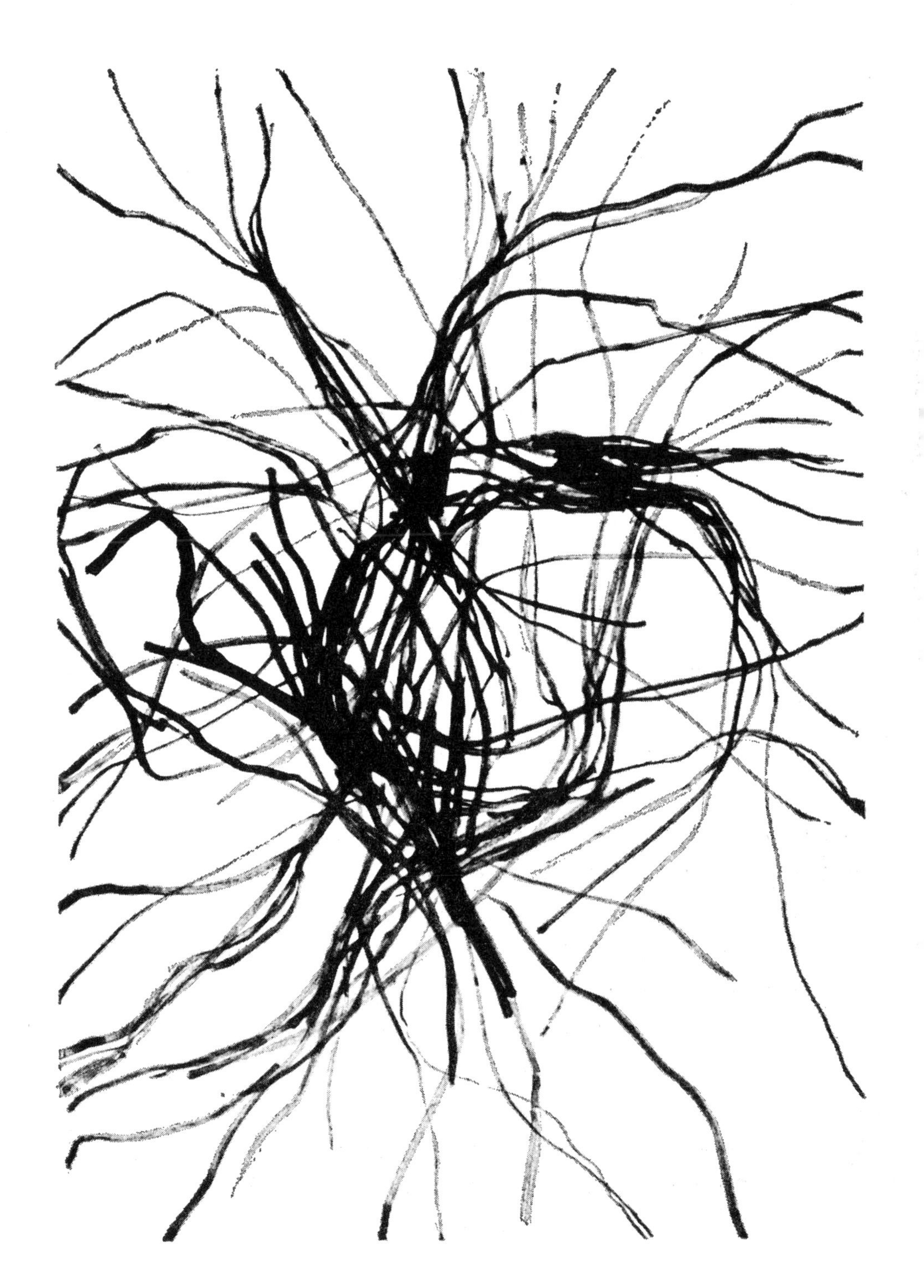

18. Drawing, 1963

19. Space Sculpture, 1957

One experiences space-time not as a scientific concept but as poetry, as one can sometimes do in a great planetarium. This development goes further and comes to a climax with No. 21. Under the first impact of this work in 1957 I wrote: 'The lines bundle, rise, then wander off in space. Their curves are not reducible to any mathematic principle. They are intuitive. The rhythm which they build is something one can hardly analyse. It comes near to the Chinese principle of the rhythm of the Universe, reinterpreted by Western science and Western sensibility.'[6]

Another product of this period is the first architectural sculpture. Thanks to the interest of Werner Ruhnau, the chief architect, it was commissioned for the City Theatre of Munster in Westphalia. It takes the form of a relief over the entrance: a double loop with one end fastened and the other free. This earned a popular nickname, 'Picasso Blitz'. 'Picasso' equals modern and 'Blitz' speed. That shows surprising sympathy. The light and flying curves lash the architectural planes as a child whips a spinning-top. The museum world in Germany was far from grasping so much at that time.

It is still often said that sculpture has no place on modern buildings. Surfaces which are not carrying walls cannot support massive reliefs. So much is obvious. An architectural structure based on stress and strain cannot use monumental work in the same way as Romanesque or Classical, which repose in themselves. Sculpture has another function now. One may be dealing with a single corner, as in Munster, or with a city precinct, as Berto Lardera is with his sculpture on the Hansa-Platz in Berlin. It is all the same. In the one case as the other, the work must absorb the architectural rhythms and give them a point of concentration.

A second architectural sculpture, No. 22, stems from the forms of 1955, though it was carried out much later on. This is not a relief but a free-standing work. Its situation is very difficult. Behind, there stands a skyscraper, the office block of the Mannesmann Company (Architect Paul Schneider-Esleben). To the left lies a massive neo-classicistic building by Peter Behrens, Germany's first modern architect. On the right is a huge side-wall, without meaning or proportion. In this stone pit the only open view is forwards, to the road, the river and the trees. A massive or a figurative work would be crushed here. Space-sculpture simply does not take up the challenge.

The Mannesmann sculpture develops in three phases: one below with strongly rising curves, the middle where they cross and mingle, and the top where they shoot apart. The time-scale one would have in music becomes simultaneous. Everything happens at once. The 'symphonic' composition so compressed achieves monumentality without the mass. The work stands to the modern

20. Space Sculpture
'Sphere', 1955

21. Space Sculpture
White 'Flowing'
1956

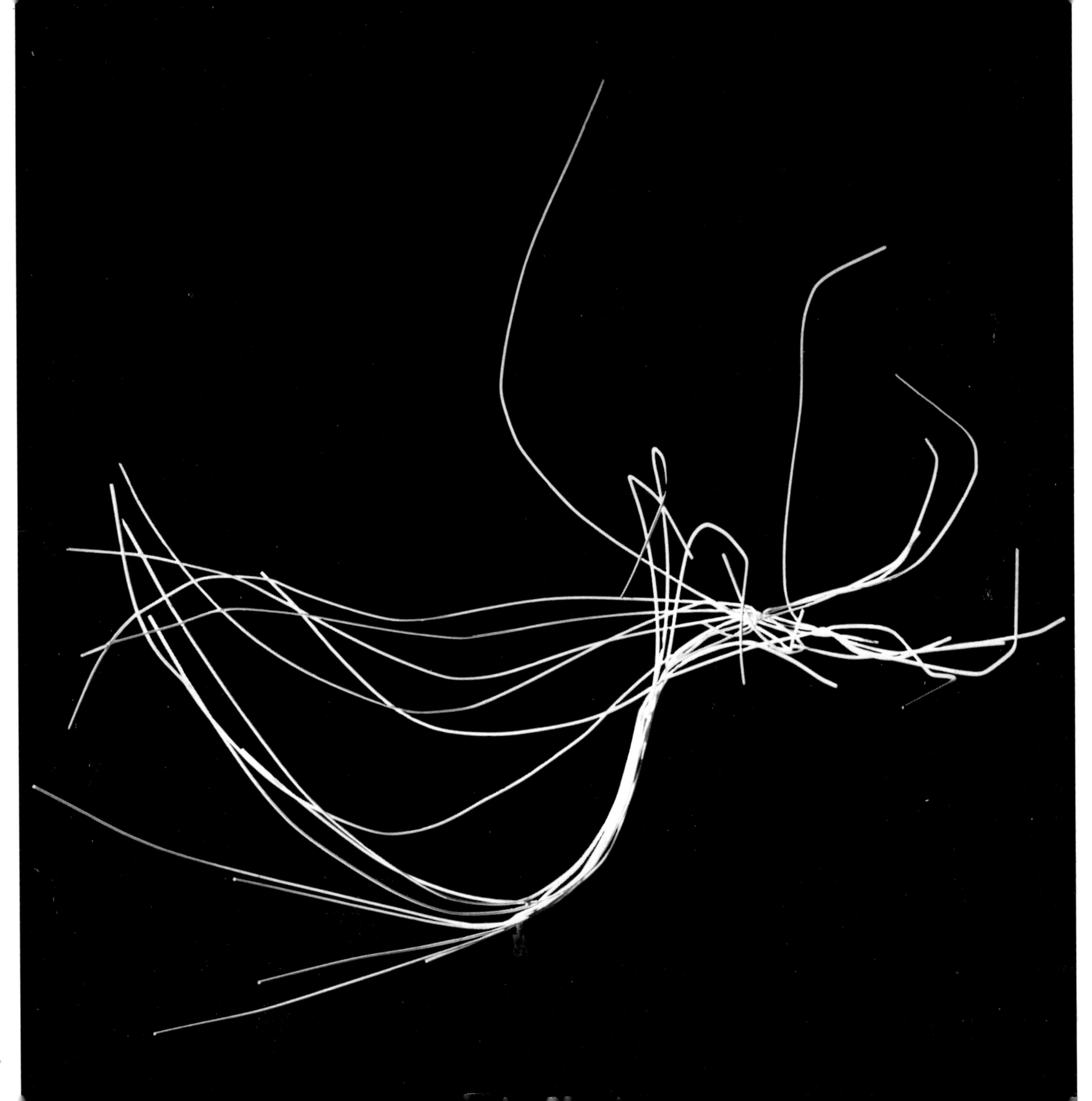

22. Space Sculpture Mannesmann, 1958–1961

city space, compressed and vertical, much as Verocchio's Colleoni monument does to the horizontal city of the early Renaissance.
At the same time as the relief in Munster, while the 'Balls-of-energy' were developing in full force, Kricke began a set of charcoal drawings. These seemed at first to contradict all he was doing. Straight, horizontal lines cover their surfaces without a break. The dimensions are often long and narrow, as in No. 23. The effect is sometimes landscape, sometimes a flat surface, never spatial – or time-spatial – in Kricke's usual way. The stimulus behind these drawings was a painting by Max Ernst (*c.* 1926) which has a linear structure, this time vertical, in yellow, red and black. Obviously the sculptor needed this as catalyst for a new vision forming in his mind. This became clear after a year or so in the new works which he called 'Flächenbahnen' or 'Plains'.

These two-dimensional sculptures are less simple than they seem. From one angle they will remind one of a tree in silhouette out of a Chinese Kakemono (No. 25). From another they have a double dynamic, seeming to go two ways at once (No. 28). When they are mounted out of doors they flash like moving light along a stream (No. 29). All Kricke's works are relatively independent of the earth. The 'Plains' are the freest of all. Yet floating often goes with architectural quality (No. 26). Such pieces remind one of Malevich, only translated from a cubic to a linear style. This double character is the basis for the big relief on the City Theatre at Gelsenkirchen in the Ruhr (No. 27).

In the decoration of this theatre, architect Ruhnau made an attempt to realize today the old idea of the collective work of art. The effect of the glass façade is heightened by the rolling forms of a relief in concrete by the English sculptor Robert Adams. Inside, the foyer is transformed by huge walls in blue monochrome and smaller sponge-reliefs in the same colour by the late Yves Klein.[7]
Kricke's field was the side-wall of the studio. This smaller theatre, built on piles, is linked with the main house. Its outer wall becomes a kind of floating plane, dramatised by the black colouring. The relief, a two-part 'Plain', stresses the tie to the big building. Its effect is graphic more than spatial, but that suits the situation here.

A second piece of work was commissioned for Gelsenkirchen, but has not up to now been carried out. On the square formed by the angle of the studio with the main house the sculptor planned his 'Water Forest'. A group of columns was to stand there, made of plexiglass and ten or twelve feet high. These would be filled with water pumped-up from below which, overflowing, runs in a thin film down the outside (Model, No. 30). There exists a written text from this time which incorporates Kricke's ideas for water. Another of the projects was worked out and named the 'Water Relief' (Model, No. 33).

Kricke's 'Plains' brought new possibilities, but they have their limitations too. They are not quite free-standing sculptures, rather double-faced reliefs. This is still so in cases such as No. 29, where one component 'sets' tangential to the rest. Yet in this tangent lies the germ of the development. Toward the end of 1958, after a break of almost a year in America, this crystallized in No. 34. This twelve-foot work was shown first at the 'documenta II' in Cassel, early the next year. It did more than anything up to that time for Kricke's international reputation.

In the spiral of development the work of this time, represented here by Nos. 34, 36, 38, 41, comes back to the early period of 1949–53. In the reach of No. 34, or in the synthesis in No. 35 of movement with the monumental, the great sense of scale returns. Meanwhile the *simplisme* limiting the early work has disappeared. The rhythmic play is subtle, even complicated now, yet the whole keeps its unity.

There is also something in addition. If one looks closely, the big 'documenta' piece (No. 34) shows a leaping figure. No. 38 again has something animal, or rather birdlike in its forms. And while the sculpture has regained its grand dimension this no longer lies, as did the early work, outside the human. Such works are the best reply to the reproach of a materialism on the one hand,[8] as to a theological interpretation on the other.[9] Like the works of Brancusi half a century ago, these are Humanistic documents, which support the words of Santayana: 'There is only one world, the natural world, and only one truth about it; but this world has a spiritual life in it, which looks not to another world but to the beauty and perfection that this world suggests, approaches and misses.'[10]

At this point, with no alteration in technique or style, there comes a sudden change. If one compares Nos. 36 and 38 with 39 and 40 which follow on, the effect is quite different. An element of conflict has entered. The rhythms contradict each other to the point that the two later pieces seem half torn apart. Yet from these clashing movements there is born a third, a spatial spiral. Meanwhile the new organic element, whether man, bird or animal, has become more pronounced. Here, for the first time, it dominates the technological. In this, something in the sculptor's private life has obviously played a part. In 1959 he started to breed carrier-pigeons – a superficial look shows the effect. The wing and tail, the plumage ruffling or smooth, the fluttering, even the position of the claws all show quite plainly. This may seem comical. But when an artist grasps at anything, however trivial, he seeks the objective correlate for something in himself. In fact the 'Pigeons on the grass, alas' play the same part as that painting by Ernst which inspired the 'Plains'.

25. Plain, drawing, 1955

24. Plain, 1956
25. Great Plain, 1959 〉

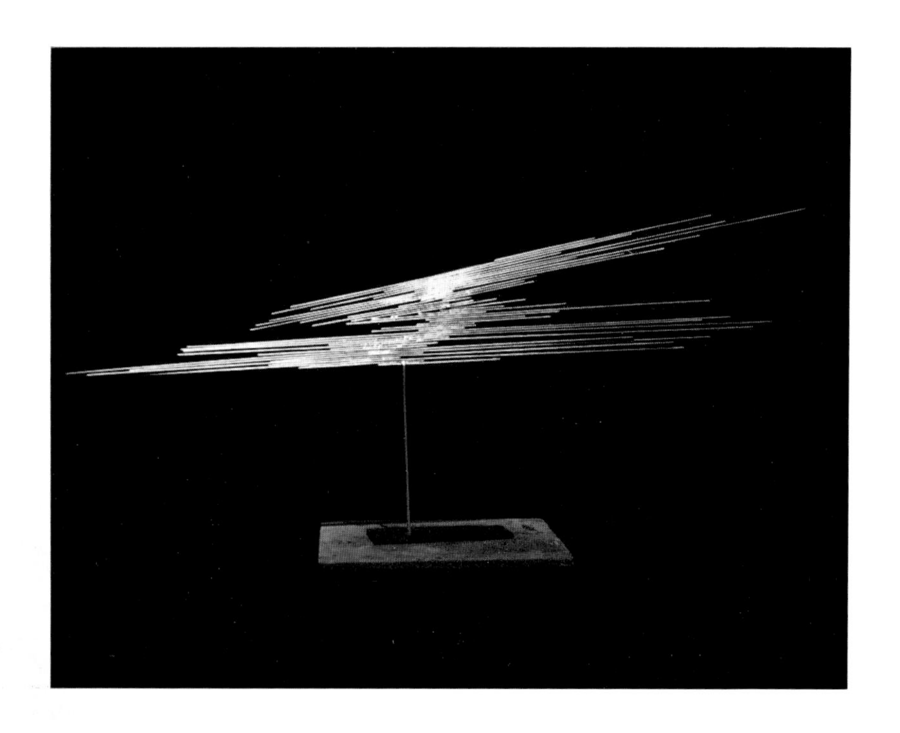

26. Plain, 1958

27. Great Relief in Two Plains, 1957–1959

28. Plain, 1956

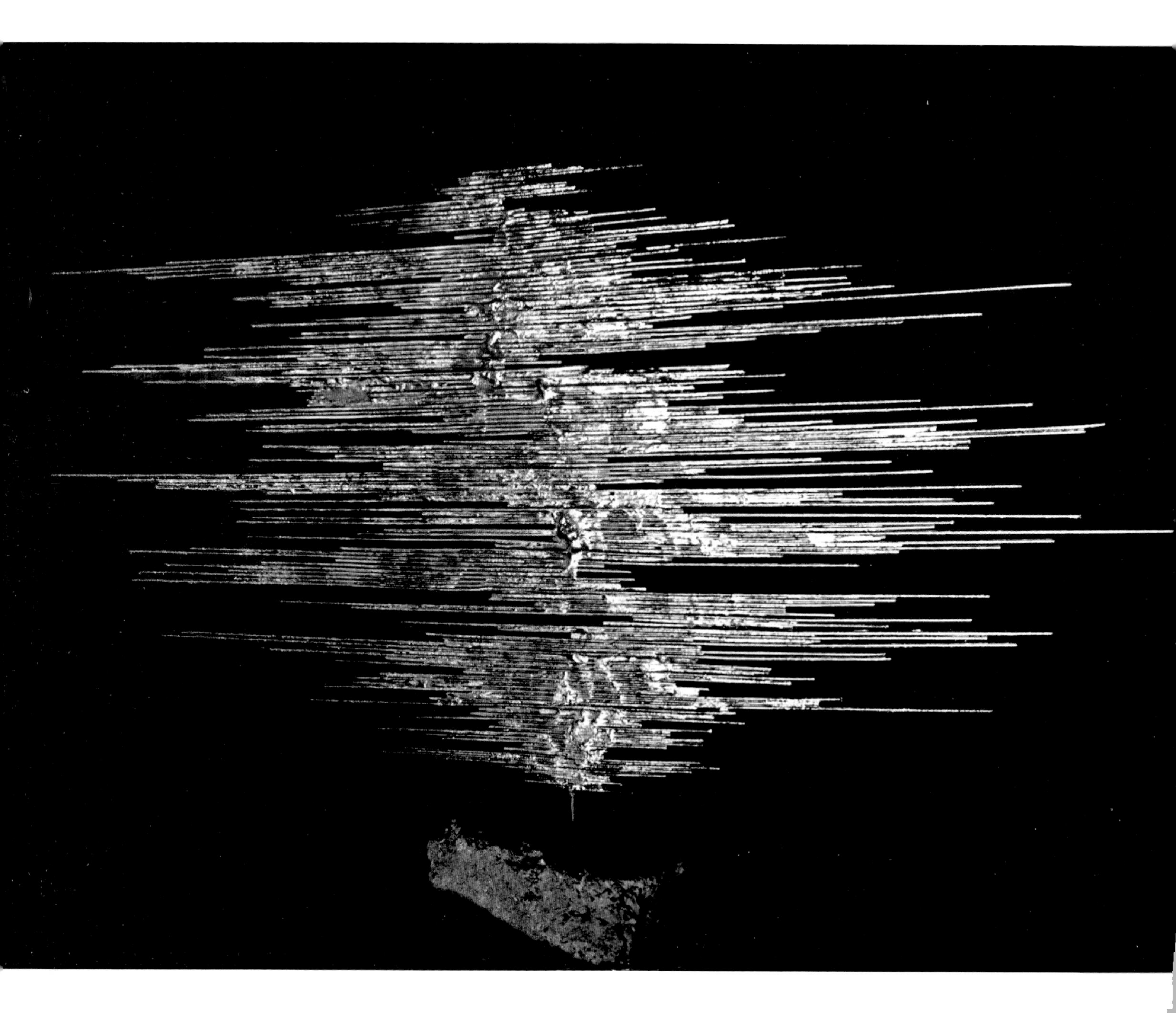

29. Plain 'Crossing', 1956

30. Water Forest, model, 1956

Several groups of ‘water columns’ are placed on the square in an asymmetrical composition.

Cylinders of plexiglass are set up. Water rises within, not spurting, but so that the overflow outside runs down the glass in a transparent and vibrating film of movement, making the material (plexiglass) disappear. At the base each column is surrounded by a narrow slot in the paving, into which the water runs unobtrusively and noiselessly.

Out of the paving, these living pillars rise, still and yet flickering with motion, and glittering with light. One can approach close to the columns and make one’s way through the ‘Forest’.

31. Water Forest, detailed plan, scale 1:10

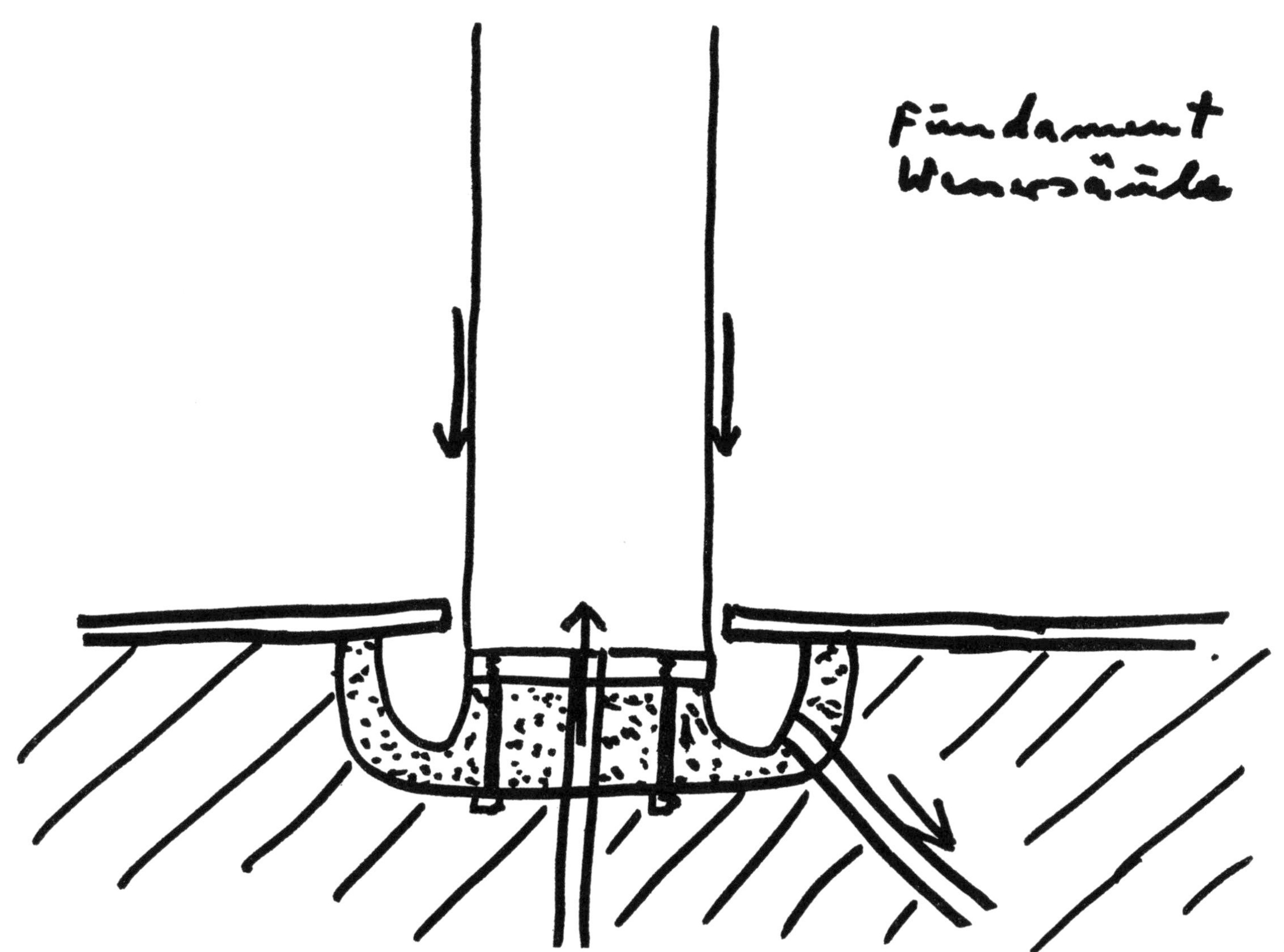

32. Water Relief, section, scale 1:200

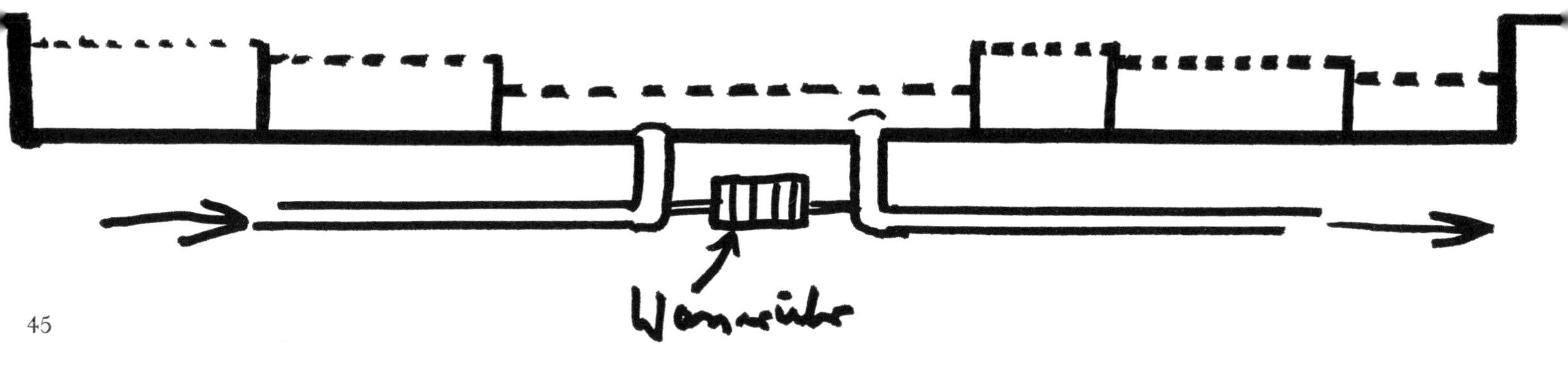

33. Water Relief, model, 1956

The basin is sunk in the earth to a depth of approximately two feet. It is divided up by thin concrete walls of various heights. These form compartments open only to the sky.

The inflow and outflow are situated at the bottom of the shallowest compartment. They are timed and regulated by means of a simple mechanical water-clock.

Initial position

At the highest level, the basin is filled to within two inches of the verge. The whole water surface is smooth and unbroken. All the walls are submerged.

Ebb

The outflow in the shallowest chamber opens and the water surface sinks slowly. One wall after another appears and each holds back, at its own height, that part of the water which it encloses. In a series of levels, one after the other, there appears a relief composed of separate surfaces of water. When the lowest of these surfaces has been reached, the outflow valve closes automatically.

Flow

The inflow opens. The water begins to rise and step by step reabsorbs one after the other of the water levels in itself. Once it arrives at the top, it again forms the unified water surface directly below the verge.

Ebb

The outflow opens and the water surface sinks . . .

35. Water Relief, model, 1956

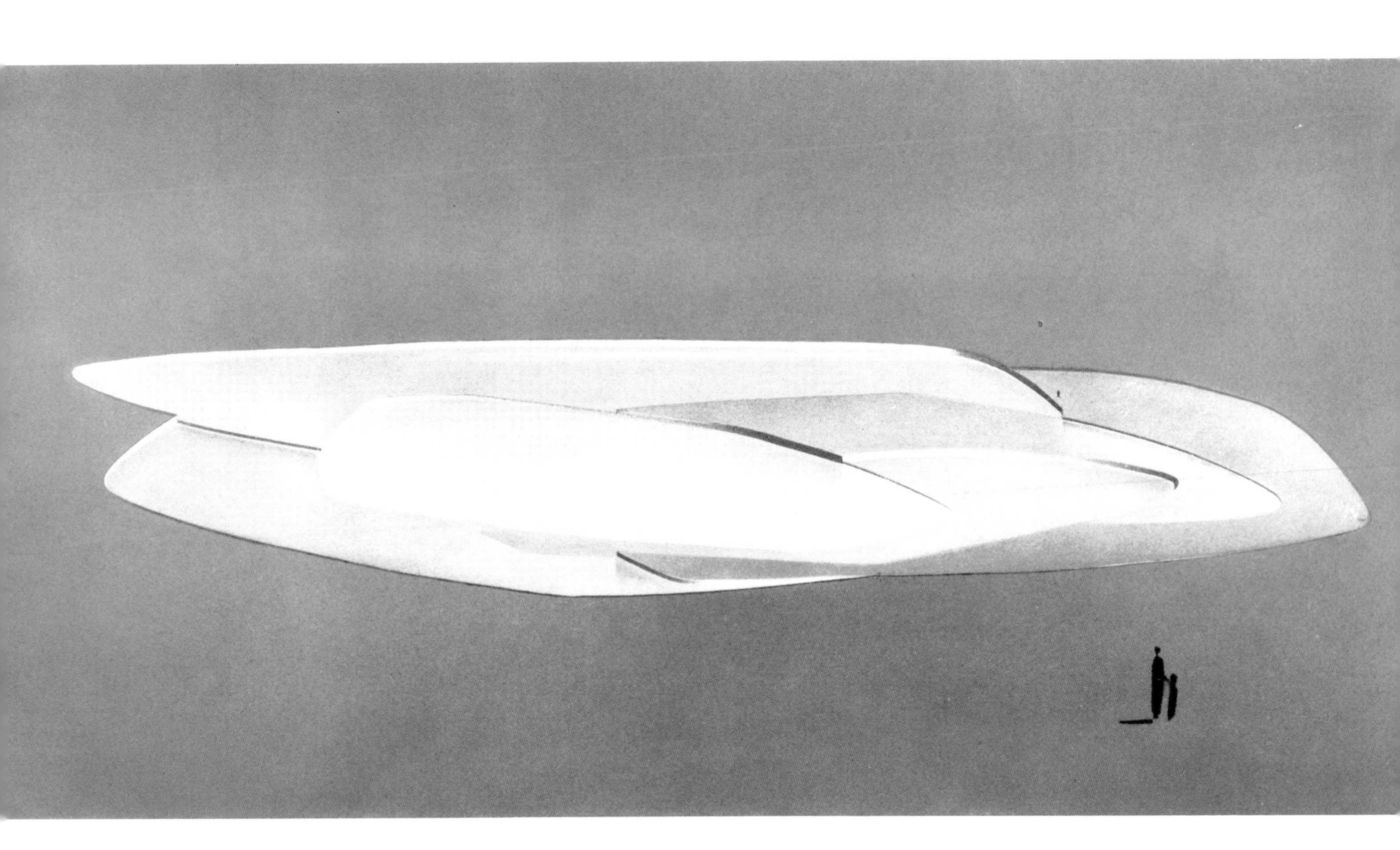

34. Space Sculpture called 'Große Kasseler' 1958–1959

35. Great Space Sculpture, 1960–1962

36. Space Sculpture, 1960

37. Drawing, 1959

38. Space Sculpture, 1960

Is that surprising? For Kricke the world of space and speed is everything. It is his world, where his imagination and his sense of form are freed. Physics and technology gave the first stimulus. They are the things which have formed our environment. Yet they are still our superficial part. All men, the artist with them, have their roots, millions of years old, in the natural world from which they came. What is the bridge between this world and that of space and movement if not – the bird?

From this period come the ideas for No. 52, a sculpture for the Rothschild park at Reux. Here the 'Plains' are piled up on top of one another. Gestures travel out in space. Bundles of polished rods flash after one another like the Jovian thunderbolts. Curves leap from different angles, twist in different ways, yet form a continuity. At the foot the lines separate and dash up again in a wave. More than three tons of steel jut up into the air and seem to have no weight whatever. The parts seem scarcely connected at all. When one has appreciated the dynamic balance, the lightness runs through one's limbs. After the speed has entered one it is transformed into stillness and silence.

Works like Nos. 44, 46 and 48–51, from Kricke's latest phase, could disappoint and confuse his former fans. Up to the 'Pigeons', the mark of his work is symmetry. A new symmetry, true, balancing speeds and not weights. But space-geometry or curves or plains are always logical, even predictable. With the 'Pigeons' it began to disappear; and this goes on. The plain is bent, its surface holed. Rods run out independently and point all ways. Fragments contort themselves. One is reminded of the moment Jackson Pollock shattered cubist order in his work and with his 'drippings' started a new kind of art.

The painter made his break for freedom into order of another kind. Has Kricke done the same? Instead of a speed-symbol, we now have a whole gamut of movement in each piece. The new sculptures are polyphonic, variable in their play with space. One can see the sculptor feeling his way in drawings like Nos. 1 and 18. But how will it go on? One possibility is shown in No. 46. This is no isolated piece and it shows very close connections with one of eight years earlier, No. 21. Or put the other way one can see No. 21 as an extraordinary *saut*, a foretaste of what was to come much later. In No. 46 just as in No. 21 the movement looks slow, like seaweed drifting under water. But the real element of both is space. In the depths of outer space, speed is comparative. Even the movement of the light takes centuries. Here if anywhere is 'pure esthetic immediacy by way of the immediately apprehended esthetic continuum of which (the artist) is a part.'[11] A relation with nature which the Oriental artist has possessed for centuries. To give it form in our world and our time seems to me as near a definition as we can get of the meaning of the work of Norbert Kricke.

39. Space Sculpture, 1959

40. Space Sculpture, 1960

41. Space Sculpture, 1961

Notes

[1] Erich Neumann: 'Art and the Creative Unconscious'. Bollingen Foundation Inc., 1959

[2] Wolfgang Groezinger: 'Scribbling, Drawing, Painting' (p. 111). Faber, London, 1955

[3] Hermann Minkowsky, 1908. Quoted by S. Giedion: 'Space, Time and Architecture'. Oxford University Press, London, 1941

[4] Quoted in exhibition catalogue 'Henri Laurens', Folkwang Museum, Essen, Germany

[5] S. Giedion. *op. cit.*

[6] Report in Arts Magazine. New York, March 1957

[7] City Theatre at Gelsenkirchen. Robert Adams and Yves Klein were both proposed by Norbert Kricke for these tasks. In addition Paul Dierkes (Berlin) worked on the 'drum'-wall which separates the auditorium from the foyer and a mobile relief by Jean Tinguely (Paris) hangs in the auditorium of the Studio

[8] Edouard Roditi: Report in Arts Magazine. New York, February 1962

[9] Otto Mauer: Speech at the opening of the Kricke exhibition in Museum Haus Lange, Krefeld, Germany, 14 October 1962

[10] Quoted by Julian Huxley: 'The Humanist Frame' (p. 48). Allen and Unwin, London, 1961

[11] F.S.C. Northrop: 'The Meeting of East and West' (pp. 317–18). Macmillan, New York, 1946

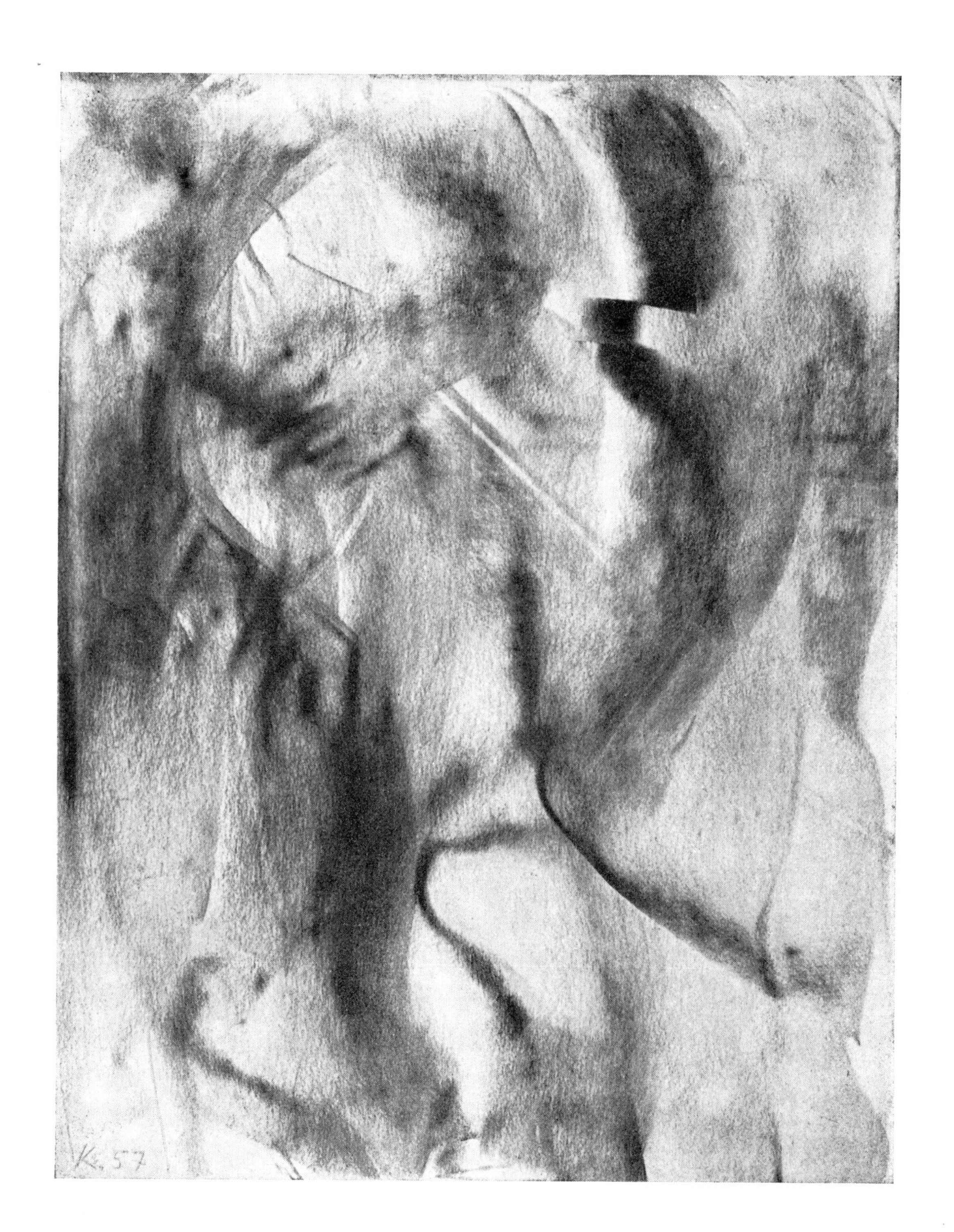

42. Drawing, 1957

45. Space Sculpture, 1959

44. Space Sculpture, 1962

45. Space Sculpture called 'Kleine Engelskirchener' 1960

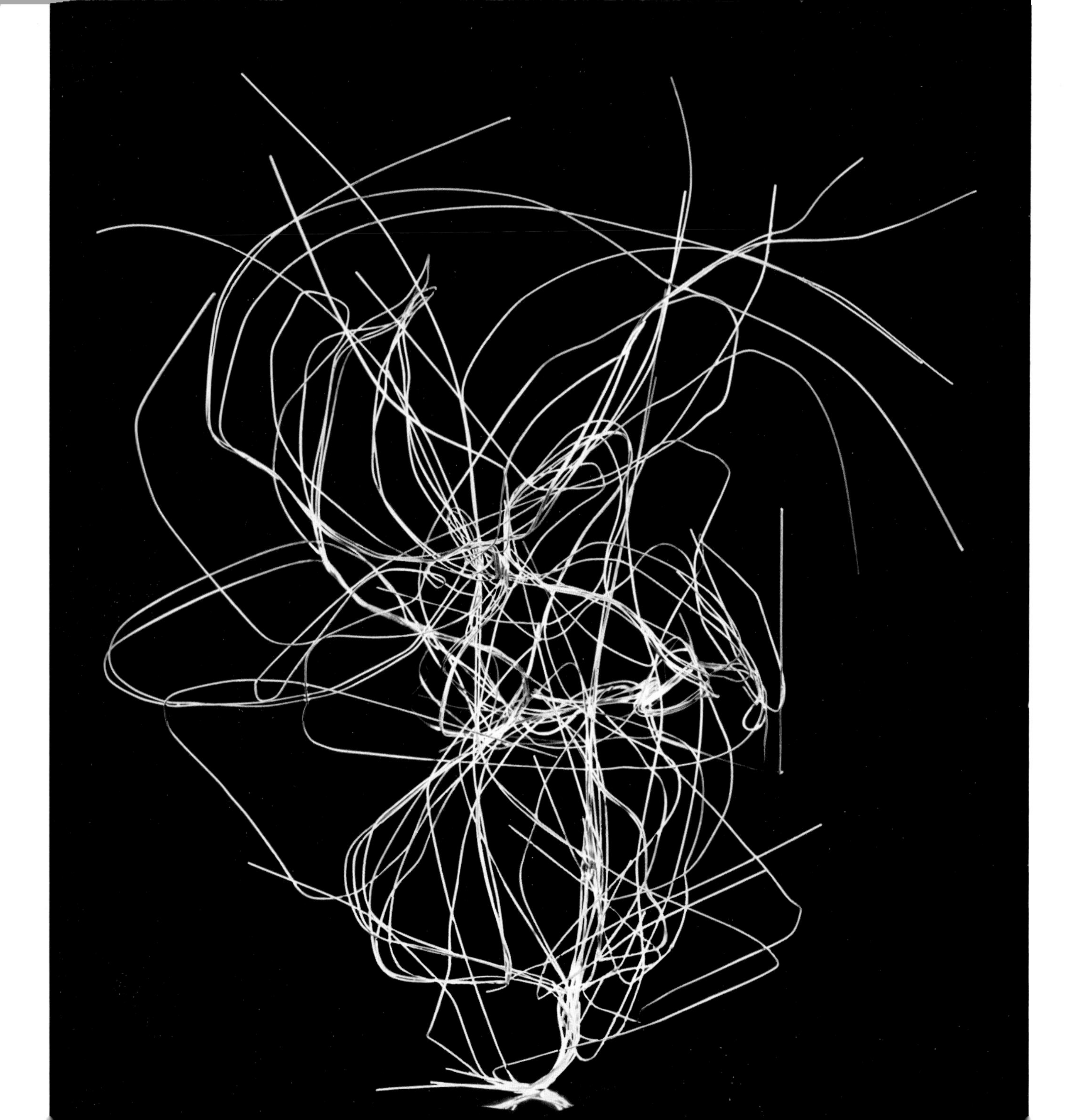

46. Space Sculpture, 1960

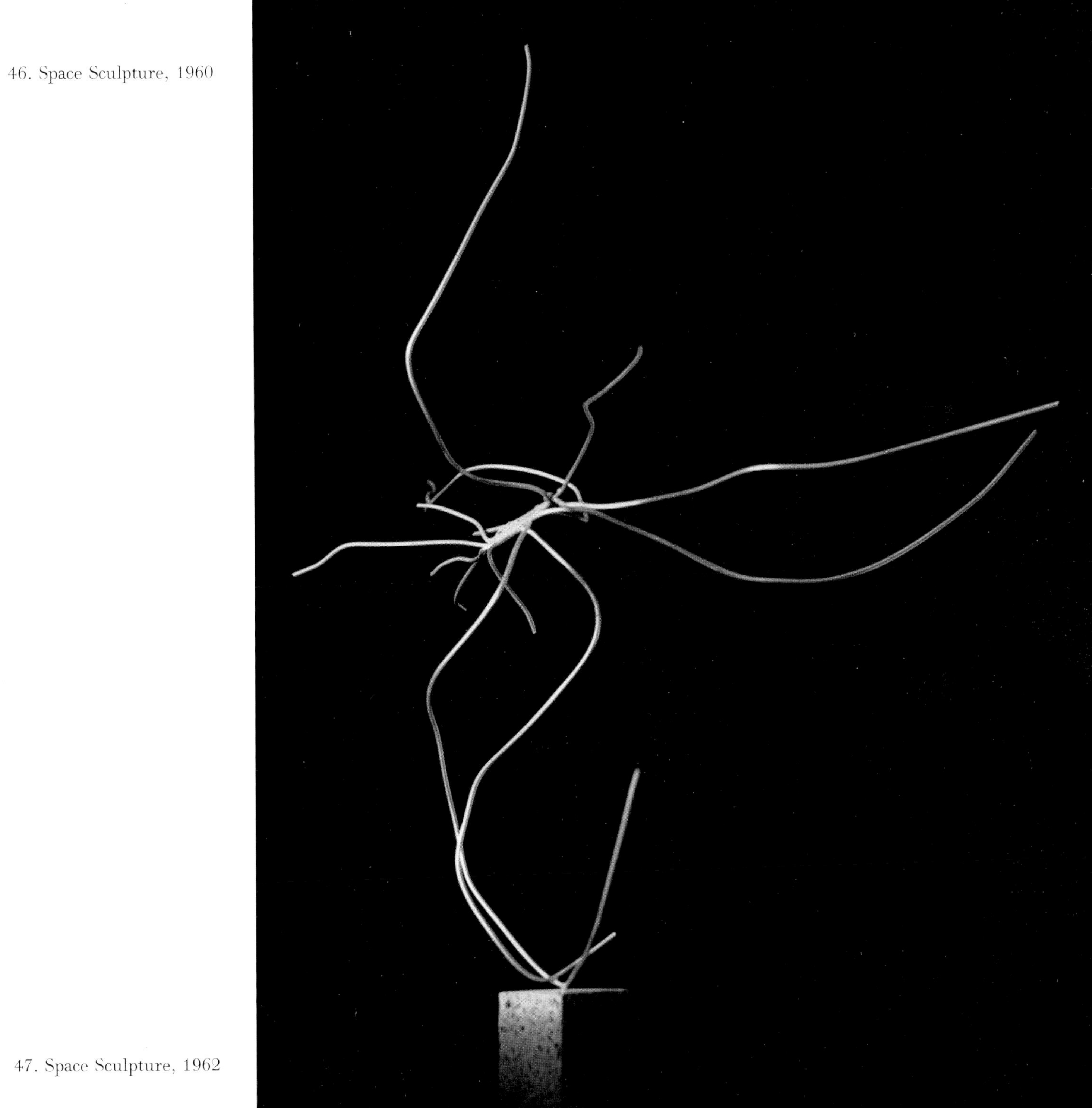

47. Space Sculpture, 1962

48. Space Sculpture
'Chi', 1961

49. Space Sculpture
1961

50. Space Sculpture
1961

51. Space Sculpture
1961

52. Space Sculpture called 'La grande de Reux' 1961–1963

List of Plates

1 Drawing, 1963. China-ink. Specially drawn for this book as a symbol of infinite space

2 Plain and Space, 1950. Steel, 26 × 43,5 × 51 cm

3 Space Sculpture Yellow-White-Black, 1956. Painted steel, 60 × 75 × 35 cm.
Coll. Herbert Paas, Düsseldorf, Germany

4 Space Sculpture, 1952. Steel painted white, 48 × 80 × 37 cm.
Kunstmuseum, Düsseldorf, Germany

5 'Small Liègeois' White-Terracotta, 1952. Painted steel, 56 × 118 × 36 cm

6 Space Sculpture Red, 1954. Iron-wire painted red, 15 × 31 × 12 cm.
Coll. Rolf Jährling, Wuppertal-Elberfeld, Germany

7 Small White Architectural, 1950. Painted steel, 26 × 14 × 12,5 cm.
Coll. Peter Powell, London

8 Space Sculpture White 'Temple', 1952. Painted steel, height 2,03 m.
Leo Castelli Gallery, New York

9 Green Curve, 1952. Painted steel, height *c.* 20 cm

10 Space Sculpture White, 1955. Painted steel, height *c.* 59 cm.
Coll. Dr Konrad Henkel, Düsseldorf, Germany

11 Space Sculpture, 1955. Nickel, height *c.* 30 cm. Coll. Peter Powell, London

12 Drawing, 1956. Charcoal. Coll. Dr W. Heits, Düsseldorf, Germany

13 Drawing, 1955. Black chalk

14 Space Sculpture, 1955. Nickel, height 42 cm

15 Space Sculpture Grey-White, 1955–1956. Painted steel, height *c.* 80 cm

16 Space Sculpture 'Hornet', 1955–1956. Nickel, 28 × 44 × 27 cm.
Coll. Dr Hanns Theodor Flemming, Hamburg

17 Space Sculpture, 1955. Nickel, 22 × 55 × 15 cm.
Coll. Gerd and Ursula Hatje, Stuttgart, Germany

18 Drawing, 1963. China-ink

19 Space Sculpture, 1957. Cadmium, height *c.* 35 cm.
Coll. Charles Murphy, Chicago

20 Space Sculpture 'Sphere', 1955. Nickel, height *c.* 35 cm.
Coll. Hans-Peter Tebartz, Wittlaer, near Düsseldorf, Germany

21	Space Sculpture White 'Flowing', 1956. Painted steel, height *c.* 75 cm
22	Space Sculpture Mannesmann, 1958–1961. Refined steel, height 7 m. Tower office block of the Mannesmann Company, Düsseldorf, Germany
23	Plain, drawing, 1955. Charcoal
24	Plain, 1956. Nickel, height *c.* 30 cm. Coll. Dr Carola Giedion-Welcker, Zürich
25	Great Plain, 1959. Steel, 115×243×0,8 cm. Coll. George W. Staempfli, New York
26	Plain, 1958. Nickel, height *c.* 24 cm. Galerie Karl Flinker, Paris
27	Great Relief in Two Plains, 1957–1959. Steel, length 34 m. City Theatre, Gelsenkirchen, Germany
28	Plain, 1956, Nickel, height *c.* 35 cm. Coll. Charles Murphy, Chicago
29	Plain 'Crossing', 1956. Steel, height *c.* 80 cm, length *c.* 230 cm. Coll. Yves Klein, Paris
30	Water Forest, model, 1956
31	Water Forest, detailed plan, scale 1:10
32	Water Relief, section, scale 1:200
33	Water Relief, model, 1956
34	Space Sculpture called 'Große Kasseler', 1958–1959. Refined steel, height 3,08 m. In possession of the town of Leverkusen, Germany
35	Great Space Sculpture, 1960–1962. Refined steel, height 3,20 m, width *c.* 4 m. Versorgungsamt Gelsenkirchen, Germany
36	Space Sculpture, 1960. Refined steel, height *c.* 55 cm. Coll. Peter Selz, New York
37	Drawing, 1959. China-ink. Hertha Kricke
38	Space Sculpture, 1960. Refined steel, height 52 cm. Lefebre Gallery, New York
39	Space Sculpture, 1959. Refined steel, height *c.* 30 cm.
40	Space Sculpture, 1960. Refined steel, height 28 cm. Lefebre Gallery, New York

41 Space Sculpture, 1961. Refined steel, height 74 cm. Coll. Edgar Faure, Paris
42 Drawing, 1957. Charcoal
43 Space Sculpture, 1959. Steel, 30×29×23 cm.
Coll. Dr Breetzke, Düsseldorf, Germany
44 Space Sculpture, 1962. Refined steel, height *c.* 35 cm. Hertha Kricke
45 Space Sculpture called 'Kleine Engelskirchener', 1960. Nickel, height *c.* 40 cm
46 Space Sculpture, 1960. Refined steel, height *c.* 60 cm.
Galerie Karl Flinker, Paris
47 Space Sculpture, 1962. Refined steel, height 42 cm
48 Space Sculpture 'Chi', 1961. Refined steel, height 60 cm.
Galerie Karl Flinker, Paris
49 Space Sculpture, 1961. Refined steel, height *c.* 50 cm.
Galerie Karl Flinker, Paris
50 Space Sculpture, 1961. Refined steel, height 59 cm.
Coll. Contessa Christina de Brandolini, Venice
51 Space Sculpture, 1961. Refined steel, height 71 cm.
Coll. Edgar Faure, Paris
52 Space Sculpture called 'La grande de Reux', 1961–1963. Refined steel,
height 7,50 m. Coll. Baroness Alix de Rothschild, Château de Reux, Normandy

The measurements are given in the order of height, width, depth.

Biography

1922	Born in Düsseldorf on 30 November; grew up in Berlin
1947	Returned to Düsseldorf
1949	First space-sculptures
1953	First exhibition at the Ophir Gallery, Munich
1954	Exhibition at the Parnass Gallery, Wuppertal, Germany
1955	Exhibition at the Düsseldorf Kunsthalle, at the Istanbul City Gallery, at the Cercle Volnay, Paris, and Berne Kunsthalle. Took part in the Middelheim Biennale
1956	Created the sculpture for the new opera house in Münster, Westphalia, Germany. Exhibition at the Samlaren Gallery, Stockholm
1957	Exhibitions at the Iris Clert Gallery, Paris, and with the Kunstverein Freiburg, Breisgau, Germany. Exhibited at the Middelheim Biennale, the Milan Triennale, and in 'Réalités Nouvelles', Paris
1958	Relief in the hall of the Lufttechnische Gesellschaft, Stuttgart, Germany; water-sculpture in Bad Salzuflen, Germany. In June he met Walter Gropius in Cambridge, Mass., and started to plan water-sculptures for the project of Baghdad University (directed by Gropius). Received the prize of the Graham Foundation for Advanced Studies in the Fine Arts, Chicago (suggested by S. Giedion, Zurich). Spent six months in New York. Exhibited in 'Sculpture' at the Claude Bernard Gallery, Paris, and at the Middelheim Biennale
1959	Exhibition at the Iris Clert Gallery, Paris. Exhibited at 'documenta II', Cassel, Germany, at the Claude Bernard Gallery, Paris, and the Staempfli Gallery, New York
1957–1960	Large relief and water-sculpture for the new opera house at Gelsenkirchen, Germany
1960	Official installation of his sculpture 'Große Kasseler' in the Leverkusen Museum, Germany. Exhibition at Berne Kunsthalle
1961	Installation of the great space-sculpture (1959–1961) in front of the tower office block of the Mannesmann Company, Düsseldorf. Large relief for the Apostel-Gymnasium, Cologne (1960–1961)

1961	Exhibitions at the Museum of Modern Art and the Lefebre Gallery, New York, as well as at the Galerie Karl Flinker, Paris
1962	Large space-sculpture in front of an administration building in Gelsenkirchen, Germany. Exhibition at the Haus Lange Museum, Krefeld, Germany. Took part in the World Exhibition, Seattle, and in the exhibition of the 20th-Century Museum, Vienna
1963	Exhibitions at the St Stephan Gallery, Vienna, and at the Karl-Ernst-Osthaus-Museum, Hagen, Westphalia, Germany. Installation of great space-sculptures (1961–1963) at Engelskirchen, Germany, and in the park of Château de Reux (Baroness Alix de Rothschild), Normandy. Won Great Sculpture Prize of North-Rhine-Westphalia, Germany

Bibliography

Hans Theodor Flemming: 'Norbert Kricke'. Quadrum 7, 1959
Carola Giedion-Welcker: 'Contemporary Sculpture: an Evolution in Volume and Space'. New York and London, rev. ed., 1961
Guy Habasque: 'Conversation dans l'atelier – Norbert Kricke'. L'Oeil no. 86, February 1962
Udo Kultermann: 'Der Bildhauer Norbert Kricke'. m + d, August 1959
Udo Kultermann: 'Norbert Kricke'. Deutsche Bauzeitung no. 9, September 1962
Gert von der Osten: 'Plastik des 20. Jahrhunderts in Deutschland, Österreich und der Schweiz'. Königstein/Taunus, Germany, 1962
Franz Roh: 'Zur Neuen Plastik in Deutschland'. Werk no. 47, 1960
Juliane Roh: 'Raumplastik von Norbert Kricke'. I 4 Soli, March/April 1956
Juliane Roh: 'Deutsche Bildhauer der Gegenwart'. Munich, 1957
Michel Seuphor: 'Sculpture of this Century'. London, 1960
John Anthony Thwaites: 'Die Raumplastiken von Norbert Kricke'. Das Kunstwerk no. 3/4, 1953
John Anthony Thwaites: 'Norbert Kricke'. The Art Quarterly no. 17, 1954 (pp. 262–271, 10 plates)
John Anthony Thwaites: 'Ich hasse die moderne Kunst'. Berlin, 1960
Eduard Trier: 'Form and Space'. London, 1961
Eduard Trier: 'Norbert Kricke'. Recklinghausen, Germany, 1963
Das Kunstwerk, 9/XV, March 1962 (9 plates)

Exhibition catalogues:

Siegfried Bröse: 'Norbert Kricke, Raumplastiken und Zeichnungen'. Kunstverein Freiburg, Germany, 1957
Carola Giedion-Welcker: 'Norbert Kricke'. Galerie Karl Flinker, Paris, 1961
Peter Selz and Carola Giedion-Welcker: 'Norbert Kricke'. The Museum of Modern Art, New York, 1961
Paul Wember: 'Norbert Kricke'. Kaiser-Wilhelm-Museum, Krefeld, Germany, 1962 (with comprehensive bibliography)

List of Photographers

Ruth Baehnisch, Düsseldorf 3, 5, 9, 11; Jean Dubout, Paris 41, 46, 47, 51; Friedrichs-Mieth, Essen 8; Inge Goertz-Bauer, Düsseldorf 22; C. Hahn 2; Thomas Höpker, Bonn *Frontispiece;* Ernst Knorr, Gelsenkirchen 35; Richard Nickel, Park Ridge, Ill. 19; Hans-J. Witkowski, Düsseldorf 27

DATE DUE

DEC 13 1995	

GAYLORD PRINTED IN U.S.A.

repaired 12/95; JA 6/99, J 4/01 all pp secure